LITTLE CATECHISM

of

THE ACT OF OBLATION

of

ST. THÉRÈSE OF THE CHILD JESUS

"We make our own this prayer of St. Thérèse: 'We beseech You, O Jesus, to let Your divine gaze rest upon a vast number of childlike souls and to choose in this world a legion of little victims worthy of Your love.'"

H.H. PIUS XI
Homily at the Mass of Canonization
of St. Thérèse of the Child Jesus

Nihil Obstat:
Eduardus Gallen,
Censor Theo. Deput.

Imprimi Potest:
Ioannes Carolus,
Archiep. Dublinen., Hiberniae Primas

Dublini, die 28 Septembris, anno 1948

SOPHIA INSITUTE PRESS
www.SophiaInstitute.com

6th printing, 2022

"A few days after my *Oblation to God's Merciful Love,* I had commenced in the choir the Way of the Cross, when I felt myself suddenly *wounded by a dart of fire* so ardent that I thought I should die. I know not how to describe that transport; there is no comparison which would make the vehemence of that flame understood. It seemed as though an invisible force plunged me wholly into fire. Oh, that fire! What sweetness! One minute, one second more, and my soul must have been set free. . . ."

ST. THÉRÈSE OF THE CHILD JESUS

"Few are the souls to receive this divine wound: those chiefly whose spirit and power is to be transmitted to their spiritual children: God bestows on the founder such gifts and graces as shall be proportionate to the succession of the order as the firstfruits of the Spirit."

ST. JOHN OF THE CROSS
The Living Flame of Love

FOREWORD

St. Paul states that the greatest of all virtues is love. The Angelic Doctor, St. Thomas Aquinas, said that "Charity is the queen of all virtues." The Mystical Doctor, St. John of the Cross, taught that "in the twilight of our existence we will be judged on love." Finally, the great Doctor of the Devout Life, St. Francis de Sales, wrote that "The measure that we should love God is to love Him without measure."

St. Thérèse of Lisieux, proclaimed one of the three women Doctors of the Universal Church, made an act of oblation to the merciful love of the good God. This, indeed, was one of the hallmarks of her attaining the heights of holiness in such a short time — only twenty-four years on earth.

On her liturgical feast day, October 1, the readings in the Liturgy of the Hours give us a glimpse into the burning fire of love that consumed the heart of St. Thérèse and show us what she considered to be her true and authentic vocation.

To undergo the excruciating pains and tortures of the martyrs was not her call, nor could her body endure long hours of fasting. Finally, she came to understand that her vocation was to "be love" within the Church. In her autobiography, St. Thérèse expresses this understanding with passion and desire:

> I knew that the Church had a heart and that such a heart appeared to be aflame with love. I knew that one love drove the members of the Church to action, that if this love were extinguished, the Apostles would have proclaimed the Gospel no longer, the martyrs would have shed their blood

> no more. I saw and realized that love sets off the bounds of all vocations, that love is everything, that this same love embraces every time and every place. In one word, that love is everlasting.
>
> Then, nearly ecstatic with the supreme joy in my soul, I proclaimed: O Jesus, my love, at last I have found my calling: my call is love. Certainly I have found my place in the Church, and You gave me that very place, my God. In the heart of the Church, my mother, I will be love, and thus I will be all things, as my desire finds its direction.

What, then, does this oblation entail for you and me? Humility. A complete trust in the merciful love of Jesus. And a constant willingness to love Jesus at all times and in all places, expressing this will concretely by ardent love for our neighbor.

The fruits of this oblation are countless: a continual purification of the soul, a higher perfection stamped on all the details of life, a constant and ever-more-enlightening effusion of truth, and quick entrance into Heaven without passing through Purgatory. (#13 of the Little Catechism).

After you meditate upon these simple but profound words, Jesus, the King of love, and Mary, whose greatest virtue was charity (supernatural love), along with St. Thérèse herself, will rejoice in your offering yourself to Jesus in oblation as a victim of His merciful love!

The last and greatest commandment of Jesus was given at the Last Supper: "Love one another as I have loved you!" Our final judgment will be determined by our trust in His merciful love.

—Fr. Ed Broom, O.M.V.

Offering

OF

St. Thérèse of the Child Jesus as a Victim of Holocaust to the Merciful Love of the Good God

O my God, Most Blessed Trinity, I desire to love You and to make You loved, to labor for the glory of Holy Church by saving souls on earth and by delivering those who suffer in Purgatory. I desire to accomplish Your will perfectly and to attain to the degree of glory which You have prepared for me in Your Kingdom; in a word, I long to be a saint, but I know that I am powerless, and I implore You, O my God, to be Yourself my sanctity.

Since You have so loved me as to give me Your only Son to be my Savior and my Spouse, the infinite treasures of His merits are mine; to You I offer them with joy, beseeching You to behold me only through the eyes of Jesus and in His Heart burning with love.

Again, I offer You all the merits of the saints in Heaven and on earth, their acts of love and those of the holy angels. Lastly I offer You, O Blessed Trinity, the love and the merits of the holy Virgin, my most dear Mother; to her I entrust my oblation, begging her to present it to You. Her Divine Son, my well-beloved Spouse, during the days of His life on earth, told us: "If you ask the Father anything in my name, He will give it to you." I am, then, certain that You will hearken to my desires. . . . My God, I know it: *the more You will to give, the more You make us desire.* Immense are the desires that I feel within my heart, and with confidence I call upon You to come and take possession of my soul. I cannot receive You in Holy

Communion as often as I would, but, Lord, are You not almighty? . . . Remain in me as in the tabernacle; never leave Your little victim. . . .

I long to console You for the ingratitude of the wicked, and I pray You to take from me the power to displease You. If, through frailty, I sometimes fall, may Your divine glance purify my soul immediately, consuming every imperfection, as fire transforms all things into itself.

I thank You, O my God, for all the graces You have showered on me, in particular for having made me pass through the crucible of suffering. With joy shall I behold You on the last day bearing Your scepter, the Cross. Since You have deigned to give me for my portion this most precious Cross, I hope I may resemble You in Heaven and see the sacred stigmata of Your Passion shine on my glorified body.

After this exile on earth, I hope to enjoy possession of You in the eternal Fatherland, but I have no wish to amass merits for Heaven. I will work for Your love alone, my sole aim being to give You pleasure, to console Your Sacred Heart, and to save souls who will love You forever.

At the close of this life, I shall appear before You with empty hands, for I ask not, Lord, that You would count my works. . . . All our good deeds are stained in Your sight. I desire, therefore, to be clothed with Your own justice and to receive from Your *love* the eternal possession of You. I crave no other throne, no other crown but You, O my Beloved.

In Your sight, time is nothing; one day is as a thousand years. You can in an instant prepare me to appear before You.

That my life may be one act of perfect love, *I offer myself as victim of holocaust to Your merciful love,* imploring You to consume me unceasingly, and to let the floodtide of infinite tenderness pent up in You flow into my soul, so that I may become a martyr of Your love, O my God.

May this martyrdom, after having prepared me to appear before You, break life's web at last, and may my soul take its flight, unhindered, to the eternal embrace of Your *merciful love.*

I desire, O my Beloved, at every heartbeat to renew this oblation an infinite number of times, till the shadows fade away and I can tell You my love eternally face-to-face.

MARIE-FRANÇOISE-THÉRÈSE DE L'ENFANT-JÉSUS ET DE LA SAINTE FACE (rel. carm. ind.)

Feast of the Most Holy Trinity,
the 9th of June, in the year of
grace, 1895

Note: The indulgenced part of St. Thérèse's Act of Oblation may be found on page 20.

TABLE OF QUESTIONS

I. Before the Oblation to God's merciful love

Enlightenment and Preliminary Ideas

II. After the Oblation to God's Merciful Love

The Duties of the Victim of Love, Her Hopes, Her Attitude Toward Suffering, Her Death of Love

Appendix

FORMULA OF THE ACT OF OBLATION TO GOD'S MERCIFUL LOVE

I. Before the Oblation to God's merciful love

Enlightenment and Preliminary Ideas

1. What is the object of this *act of oblation?*

It is to compensate the good God for the refusal that His creatures oppose to the love that He desires to shower upon them.

2. How may we make this compensation to God?

By offering our hearts, so that "He may let the floodtide of His *infinite tenderness* flow over them."[1]

3. Does not this act aim at other intentions?

Many others are mentioned, it is true, but they are all included in the essential object we have just stated.

St. Thérèse of the Child Jesus says on this point: "I will work for Your love alone, *my sole aim being to give You pleasure, to console Your Sacred Heart,* and to save souls who *will love You forever.*"

It should be remarked that her desire to save souls is but a secondary intention; for if she wishes to save them, it is less for their personal happiness than to procure more love for the good God.

4. What is the origin of this act?

St. Thérèse of the Child Jesus tells us in her autobiography:

---

1 All quotations without references are drawn from the textual words of St. Thérèse of the Child Jesus or from fragments of her writings.

"In the year 1895, I received the grace to understand better than ever how much Jesus desires to be loved.

"Thinking one day of those who offer themselves as victims to the justice of God in order to turn aside the punishment reserved for sinners by taking it upon themselves, I felt this offering to be noble and generous, but I was far from feeling drawn myself to make it.

"O my Divine Master," I cried in the depths of my heart, "shall Your justice alone receive victims of holocaust? Has not Your *merciful love* also need of them? On all sides it is ignored, rejected . . . the hearts on which You would pour it out turn to creatures, seeking happiness in miserable and fleeting affections instead of casting themselves into Your arms, into the ineffable furnace of Your infinite love.

"O my God, must Your love remain disdained within Your Heart? It seems to me that if You should find souls offering themselves as *victims of holocaust to Your love,* You would quickly consume them, that You would be glad not to repress the flames of *infinite tenderness* pent up within You. . . .

"If Your justice — the justice You exercise on earth — be satisfied to discharge itself on voluntary victims, how much the more must Your *merciful love* desire to enkindle souls, since Your mercy reacheth even to the heavens.

"O Jesus, *that I may be that happy victim,* consume Your holocaust in the fire of Divine Love."

5. Why the expression *merciful love*?

Mercy, according to the graceful Latin etymology given by St. Augustine, *miseriscordare,*[2] means "to give one's heart to the wretched."

2 Fillion, *Commentaire* S. Matt. (Grande Bible).

The soul, then, that offers herself to the *merciful* love of God appeals by her very miseries to that inexplicable tendency of the Divine Heart, which inclines irresistibly to outpour its mercy without measure on the abject and the lowly.

6. In what dispositions should the soul be found who desires to draw down to herself this *merciful love*?

In a disposition of *trustful humility*. The soul should offer herself to the good God as an *empty vessel* so that He may let the floodtide of His love flow into it; or as a fire ready set, waiting for His kindling, that His torrent of flames may consume her as she desires.

7. Should the soul not first try to correct her faults, or at least to improve herself in some way?

No, it is not necessary. She gives herself just as she is, without preparation. It is useless to want to begin by having a perfect fruit—by removing its defects beforehand. *Love,* in cooperation with her goodwill, *will do this work.*[3]

8. Why the word *victim*?

By the word *victim,* St. Thérèse meant to denote a *complete oblation of herself* to the divine love; she desired that all personal life should disappear, as though it were absorbed by this love.

Again, she used the expression *victim of love* in opposition to *victim of justice* in a spontaneous outburst from her sensitive heart; she did not wish the most

3 Isa. 1:25: "And I will turn my hand to thee, saith the Lord, and will clean purge away thy dross."

beautiful attribute of God to be less favored than the other, which has long had its victims.

9. What is meant by the word *holocaust*?

Holocaust, to the saint's mind, means that the soul, "plunged in the rapturous fire of God's infinite love," aspires, ardently desires, to be *wholly consumed* and to be so transformed as to *become fire* herself at the permanent contact of the divine fire.

10. Doubtless this is what she calls a *martyrdom*?

According to the expression of St. Thérèse, the martyrdom of her life is the state of soul created by the *infinite tenderness* of God *overflowing* without measure into a human heart necessarily limited.

"I implore You," she says, "to let the floodtide of infinite tenderness pent up in You *overflow* into my soul, so that I may become a martyr of Your love, O my God!"

She completes the expression of her thought: "May this martyrdom, after having prepared me to appear before You, break life's web at last."

This disproportion, between the *infinite* tenderness of God and the *finite* heart of the poor little creature, will one day break the frail web: it is the death of love.

11. But may we not think in our humility, "I am not called to those heights; that act is not for me"?

Listen to St. Thérèse: "It is my very *weakness* that emboldens me to offer myself as a victim to Your love, O Jesus." And again: "*The weaker and more miserable we are,* the better are we *fitted* for the operations of this consuming and transforming love."

And it may be said that Thérèse — like Jesus — came to win to God's merciful love "not the just, but sinners."[4]

"In the days of old," exclaims our saint, "victims pure and without blemish were alone acceptable to the great and all-powerful God; to satisfy divine justice, perfect victims must be offered. But to the law of fear has succeeded the law of love, and Love has chosen me for a holocaust, chosen me, a weak and imperfect creature! And is this choice not worthy of love? Yes, *that Love may be fully satisfied, it must come down to nothingness and transform this nothingness into fire.*"

Let us remember that "what Thérèse did, all little souls may do." Did she not say: "O Jesus, I feel that were it possible to find a weaker soul than mine You would take delight in showering upon her still greater favors"?

12. Has not the soul who makes the act of oblation a secret hope of reward?

Our saint replies in the formula itself of the act: "I have no wish to amass merits for Heaven. . . . At the close of this life, I shall appear before You with *empty hands,* for I ask not, Lord, that You would count my works."

Again she says in her *Story of a Soul:* "It is not the riches and glory, even the glory of Heaven, that my heart seeks; *what I ask for is love.*"

It is not to seek her own beauty that she begs our Lord to consume at once all her imperfections in the fire of His love. It is solely that she may retain the privilege of being able *to give Him joy,* of making some compensation to His Divine Heart: "*I long to console You for the ingratitude*

4 Matt. 9:13.

of the wicked, and I pray You take from me the power to displease You. If, through frailty, sometimes I fall, may Your divine glance purify my soul immediately, consuming every imperfection — as fire transforms all things into itself."

13. Does not this act nevertheless obtain for the soul some personal advantages?

Yes, although our saint did not seek them directly, her motives being far removed from all personal interest. These are, in her own thought, the principal advantages:

1. A continual purification of the soul, whose imperfections are constantly consumed by love: "Ah! Since that happy day of my oblation," writes St. Thérèse, "love penetrates and surrounds me; *at each moment* this merciful love renews and *purifies me,* leaving in my heart no trace of sin."
2. A higher perfection stamped on all the details of life: "When a soul is wholly consecrated to love, *all her actions,* even the most indifferent, are marked by this divine seal."
3. A constant and ever-more-enlightening effusion of truth — i.e., of humility — for this love is *light* as well as heat. "My soul is *all shining* and gilded," declared St. Thérèse, "because it is exposed to *the rays of love.* If this Divine Sun withheld from me His rays, my soul would immediately become obscured and enveloped in darkness."

   This light preserves in the soul the sense, ever more relished, of her littleness, her nothingness, and at the same time, of the divine mercy. The soul feels with our saint: "What pleases God — better than the most generous aspirations — is to see me love my *littleness* and my *poverty;* my *blind trust in His mercy.* This is my only treasure."

4. After having lived her life of love, "the soul will take her flight, *unhindered,* to the eternal embrace of God's merciful love, therefore, without passing through Purgatory." St. Thérèse promises that "for victims of love there will be no judgment, but rather the good God will hasten to reward with eternal delights the love for Him that He will see burning in their hearts. *The fire of love is more sanctifying than the fire of Purgatory.*"

14. Does not this act also arouse a zeal for souls?

Yes, it procures for the soul surrendered unreservedly to divine love an immense apostolic influence; and this by virtue of the privileged place that the act rightly wins for her in the bosom of the Church.

"In the heart of my Mother, the Church, I shall be love," may the soul repeat with St. Thérèse. Thanks to it, "she will be all," contributing everywhere and in all times to all the advances and victories on the mission field. "*Love comprises all vocations.*" Love alone is the motive-power for all the members of the Church. It embraces *all times* and *all places,* because it is eternal.

The efficacy of its hidden influence cannot be surpassed by any other activity. Our saint likes to assure us with St. John of the Cross that "the smallest act of pure love is of greater value to the Church than all other works united together."[5]

5 *Spiritual Canticle.*

15. Will all the victims of love share in the same privileges?

All victim-souls are consumed, transformed by love, and irradiate it, but *only in the proportion in which they surrender themselves,* that is, according as they allow to divine love full freedom and all its intensity of action. St. Thérèse forewarns her disciples: "The soul is consumed by love *only insofar as she surrenders herself to love.*"

But just as "in the Father's house there are many mansions,"[6] so may there also be many degrees in the donation of oneself. . . . If all souls, victims of love, have a place in love's furnace, it is possible, nevertheless, that some do not fully expose themselves to its flames. Yet they have more graces than those who never entered it; God surrounds them with a special tenderness up to the last moment of their exile. For those who put no limit to the effusion of divine love, the good God will also, as for St. Thérèse, work "wonders that will infinitely surpass their immense desires."

16. Will these *perfect* victims of love be very many?

They may be *legion,* since St. Thérèse — and with her the Vicar of Jesus Christ Himself, His Holiness Pius XI, in the course of the solemn function of her canonization — implored the Lord to "choose out a *legion* of little Victims *worthy* of His love." Our saint has besides assured us that "all her hopes would be realized."

6 John 14:2.

17. Might it not be preferable, through fear of infidelity, to renounce entering the legion of childlike souls, victims of love?

Certainly not, no more than the Holy Church renounces to confer Baptism on a child of whose perseverance there is no assurance. On the contrary, the Church enrolls that child in her ranks, happy to have marked him with the seal of the Redemption, to have immersed one of the redeemed in the fountain of grace. Thus, also, the oblation as victim to the merciful love of God remains a source of abundant blessings for the soul who enters the *legion* with a sincere heart, be it but for a moment.

If, however, in addition to the merit of the act, we wish to add that of obedience, and thus have an assured guide in this undertaking—which it would be regrettable to perform lightly—it may be wise to consult a director; his approval will always be a great security, and his encouragement strength for the faithful soul.

"In those days I will raise up a *poor* and *lowly* people that shall *trust* in the name of the Lord."[7]

7 Cf. Soph. 3:12.

II. AFTER THE OBLATION TO GOD'S MERCIFUL LOVE

The Duties of the Victim of Love, Her Hopes, Her Attitude toward Suffering, Her Death of Love

18. What is the interior disposition essential in order to live as a fervent victim of love?

St. Thérèse replies: "The desire alone to be victim will suffice," a sincere and persevering desire, sustained by the firm hope of obtaining from the good God, together with a full effusion of His love, all the graces necessary to return Him love for love. It is in this sense that the victim of love repeats with St. Thérèse, in her act of oblation: "I am *certain* that You will hearken to my desires. . . . My God, I know it: *the more You will to give, the more You make us desire.*"

19. But what is the soul's part of the work — her *active* cooperation with the merciful love?

The soul-victim of love has a double task to fulfill: one very active, the other apparently passive, but not less generous.

Her first duty is to aim at an ever-increasing *humility,* to strive unceasingly to clear her heart of encumbrances, to maintain it absolutely *empty* of confidence in self, and all vain seeking after creatures. "We must consent to remain always poor and without strength; there lies the difficulty, for where shall be found the truly poor in spirit? He must be sought afar off,[8] that is to say, in lowliness, in nothingness."

8 Cf. Thomas à Kempis, *Imitation of Christ*, 2, 11, 4.

"In order to enjoy the treasures of merciful love," she says elsewhere, "we must humble ourselves, must acknowledge our nothingness, and that is what many souls are not willing to do."

The second duty for the soul-victim is to tend ever more and more to "the *self-abandonment* of the little child who sleeps without fear in her Father's arms." This attitude of spiritual childhood rightly deserves the name of *victim,* for "nothing so completely *immolates self* in man as to become sincerely little."[9]

St. Thérèse is not afraid to affirm that "this abandonment *alone* really surrenders the soul into the arms of Jesus" and thus allows His love to act freely and according to the full extent of its force. That is why, in her challenge to the soul weaker than her own, she confidently asserts that it will receive favors still greater than those showered on herself, provided that the soul *abandon herself* with full confidence to the infinite mercy of the good God.

20. What are the most serious obstacles to this fervent life of love?

The author of the *Imitation of Christ* replies with St. Thérèse: "So soon as a man seeketh himself doth he fall away from love."[10] That is so because we refurnish our hearts, they are no longer empty, and the place offered to love is thereby diminished. . . . The *Imitation* also adds: "Whosoever is not ready to suffer all things and to stand resigned to the will of his Beloved, is not worthy to be called a lover."[11]

---

9 Msgr. Gay.

10 *Imitation of Christ*, 3, 5, 7.

11 Ibid., 3, 5, 8.

21. Does that mean that the real victims of love will never grow weak, at least on those two points?

No, and St. Thérèse herself reassuringly tells us so. "True," she says, "one may fall, one may not be always faithful; but love, knowing how to *draw profit from all,* very quickly consumes whatever may displease Jesus, leaving naught but profound and humble peace in the depths of the soul."

The soul then can find herself below her aspirations without ceasing to be very pleasing to the good God. If at each fall she has recourse to sincere humility, she progresses in fervor, for love finds in her the empty vessel it seeks. Our saint confidently assures us: "In an act of love, even though not felt, all is repaired, and *more than repaired.*"

22. What, then, will be the means by which the victim of love may attain to sanctity?

The soul-victim depends solely and in all circumstances on *love,* hoping for all virtue from the infinite power and liberality of this merciful love, to which she has given herself without reserve. She knows her "inability to ascend by her own efforts even the first steps of the ladder of sanctity," but she "knows whom she has believed,"[12] and she repeats to our Lord according to the formula of her act of oblation: "I long to be a saint, but I know that I am powerless, and I implore You, O my God, to be *Yourself* my sanctity. . . . All our good deeds are stained in Your sight. I desire, therefore, to be clothed with Your own justice, and *to receive from Your love* the eternal possession of You."

12 Cf. 1 Cor. 12:31.

23. And from what source here below will this constant life of love be nourished?

The divine source from whence the soul-victim will draw life will be Holy Communion; this is the unrivaled invention of the merciful love of the good God, ever eager to intermingle with human misery. By her act of oblation, St. Thérèse desired to see this mysterious and incomparable "fusion" prolonged and intensified during every moment of her life, saying to God with humble daring: "With confidence I call upon You to come and take *possession* of my soul. I cannot receive You in Holy Communion as often as I would, but, Lord, are You not almighty? . . . Remain in me as in the tabernacle; never leave Your little victim."

24. By what external sign will the sincerity of this life of love be revealed?

By a constant increase of real *fraternal charity;* this is the inevitable effect of a sincere love of God.

St. Thérèse confides to us that it was after her oblation to merciful love she received the grace "to understand in its full extent the great precept of charity." "I made it my study above all else to love God," she explains, "and it is in loving *Him* that I gradually discovered the secrets of His new commandment: that we love one another as Jesus Himself loved us."[13] And she verified it in practice day by day. "The more united I am to Jesus, the more also do I love all my Sisters." After her, the true victim of holocaust delivered up to the consuming fire of Divine Love may repeat: "Since this sweet flame consumes my heart, I run with delight, O my God, in the way of Your new commandment."

13 Cf. John 13:34.

25. Does the victim of love devote herself by virtue of her act to exceptional sufferings?

She aims only at *love,* "the more excellent gift."[14] She abandons herself to the *merciful* love of the good God — that is to say, love, tender and compassionate — without any other desire than to love Him and make others love Him, without thinking of herself or of what might happen to her.

"It is the child who surrenders herself to the will of her Father, *to suffer or enjoy according to the good pleasure of His love.*"[15]

26. Had St. Thérèse in view, then, a disposition more perfect than the desire of suffering?

Yes, and from the first lines of the Act of Oblation she specifies it: "I desire, O my God, to accomplish *Your will* perfectly."

At the end of her life, our saint confirms her opinion on this point: "I know not now how to ask anything eagerly, save the perfect accomplishment of *God's designs* upon my soul. . . . I no longer thirst for either suffering or death. . . . Long did I call upon them as the harbingers of joy. . . . Now it is the spirit of *self-abandonment* alone that guides me; no other compass have I." And on her deathbed she repeats: "I do not like one thing more than the other. *Whatever God prefers* and chooses for me — that is what I like best. *It is what He does that I love.*"

14 1 Cor. 12:31.

15 "Not impossible to be a saint." — Carmel of Lisieux.

27. Is it on that account that our saint calls the victim of love a "happy victim"?

Yes, it is just because this self-abandonment, "delicious fruit of love,"[16] is sweetness even in suffering. Love, indeed, makes sweet that which is most bitter."[17] Doubtless "it has its times of trial as well as its times of enjoyment,"[18] but it always possesses the singular privilege of being able to transform sorrow into joy, a nonsensitive joy perhaps, as this Love itself, but "superior to all joy." This is what St. Thérèse had experienced when she used to sing: *"Yes, suffering borne with love is happiness most pure. . . . My joy is to love suffering."*

It is this *perfect* joy — exquisite flower of love — that she foresees as the lot of the happy victims of her legion. This she wishes to bequeath to her sisters as a last pledge of her fraternal tenderness: "I do not promise you that you will be spared trials," she told them before departing for Heaven, "but I shall make you love them, and you will come to say with me: Thou hast given me, O Lord, delight in Thy doings [Ps. 91:5]."

28. In a word, may we not conclude that the act of oblation to God's merciful love obtains true happiness for the soul-victim?

Yes, the soul-victim, calling down upon herself the "infinite tenderness of the good God," has everything to gain in interior peace and joy; for divine love invading a human heart cannot but bring to it all the germs of happiness.

---

16 St. Augustine.

17 *Imitation of Christ,* 3, 5.

18 Reflection on *Imitation of Christ,* 3, 5.

Moreover, the act of oblation in surrendering the soul to the mercy of God's *merciful* love guarantees that this love "will have compassion on her weakness, will treat her — at every turn throughout all the vicissitudes of her exile — with tenderness, with *mercy*" and a sovereign liberality.

St. Thérèse proclaimed it in that last trial,[19] which on her own avowal took from her "all feeling of enjoyment. Never did I so feel that the Lord is sweet and merciful." And already gone down into the anguish and shadow of death, she still repeated like a song of victory: "No, I am not sorry for having surrendered myself to divine love; on the contrary . . ."

29. *To die of love,* would that mean, then, to die in transports of joy?

If a death of love implies for the soul-victim a fundamental disposition of peace and loving confidence, yet it does not suppose the suppression of the sufferings that are in death the tribute of sin.

St. Thérèse, who received a very large share of redemptive sufferings, calls our attention to this: "Our Lord died in anguish on the Cross, and yet His was the most glorious death of love ever known. *To die of love is not to die in transports of joy.*" She made a point of warning her sisters of this at the beginning of her illness: "Do not be troubled," she told them, "if I suffer much, and if you see in me no sign of happiness at the moment of my death. Our Lord died indeed a victim of love, and see the agony He endured!"

19 *Story of a Soul,* ch. 9.

The sufferings of the last moments are dispensed to each soul differently according to the designs of divine wisdom. But they are nevertheless made lighter for the victim of love by the certainty that He in whom she has blindly trusted "will grant her courage in proportion to her sufferings." "I have no fear," she has a right to repeat with St. Thérèse. "If my sufferings increase He will at the same time increase my patience."

30. What, then, is the meaning of the expression *to die of love*?

According to the mind of St. Thérèse, and without presuming to explain what must remain the secret of divine mercy, the expression *to die of love* means that at the final hour God will *let the ocean of His infinite tenderness flow in torrents* on the victim of holocaust; thus will He "prepare her in an instant to appear before Him, *and will suddenly break the slender web of her life*[20] *under the pressure of His love.*

Because it is the hour of *extreme misery* for all the children of Adam, this hour of distress will appeal to the *merciful love* of the heavenly Father and cause an outpouring of His infinite tenderness beyond all measure on the little victim, to the point of transforming her into itself in an eternal embrace.

This death wholly of love, magnificent conclusion to an earthly existence, is not necessarily felt or externally manifested; there may be no outward signs of joy or even of full consciousness or devotion.

But how may we not infallibly believe it to take place, when the faithful victim shall have *hoped for it from the*

20 Expression of our saint borrowed from St. John of the Cross.

mercy of the good God? For He is magnificent in His rewards — "able to do all things more abundantly than we desire or understand,"[21] and to "hope for great things from Him is to glorify Him."[22]

21 Eph. 3:20.

22 St. John of the Cross.

APPENDIX

31. To be a true *victim of love,* is it necessary to recite frequently the act of oblation composed by St. Thérèse of the Child Jesus?

No. St. Thérèse assures us that "prayer is an outburst from the heart; a simple glance darted upward to Heaven"; she also says in the act itself: "I desire, O my Beloved, *at every heartbeat* to renew this oblation an infinite number of times," which does not suppose the recitation of any words.

The full donation of the victim of love is, therefore, above all "a disposition of the heart." This does not depend on a more or less frequent use of any set form of prayer.

Nevertheless, Holy Church invites the faithful not alone to realize this act of oblation, but also to assimilate the thoughts and even the words of St. Thérèse; for this purpose she has enriched with precious indulgences the text of the prayer which burst forth from the heart of the saint under the inspiration of the Holy Spirit.

These are the indulgences attached in perpetuity to the recitation of the act of oblation composed by St. Thérèse of the Child Jesus, from the words: "That my life may be one act of perfect love . . ."

1. Three hundred days' indulgence each time the faithful recite this act of oblation with fervent and contrite heart.
2. A plenary indulgence once a month on the ordinary conditions to those who shall have daily recited the act.

Given at Rome (S. Penitentiary)
July 31, 1923

FORMULA OF THE ACT OF OBLATION TO GOD'S MERCIFUL LOVE

(The Indulgenced Part)

"That my life may be one act of perfect love, I offer myself as victim of holocaust to Your merciful love, imploring You to consume me unceasingly and to let the floodtide of infinite tenderness pent up in You flow into my soul, so that I may become a martyr of Your love, O my God!

May this martyrdom, after having prepared me to appear before You, break life's web at last, and may my soul take its flight, unhindered, to the eternal embrace of Your merciful love.

I desire, O my Beloved, at every heartbeat to renew this oblation an infinite number of times, till the shadows fade away and I can tell You my love eternally face-to-face.